APPETIZERS & SNACKS RECIPES

Perfect Spinach Artichoke Dip
(Total Time: 15 Min| Serves: 10)

Ingredients

- 10 oz frozen spinach, thawed
- 1 tsp onion powder
- 3 garlic cloves, chopped
- 1/2 cup mayonnaise
- 1/2 cup sour cream
- 14 oz can artichoke hearts
- 1/2 cup vegetable broth
- 8 oz mozzarella cheese, shredded
- 16 oz parmesan cheese, shredded
- 8 oz cream cheese

Directions:

1. Add all ingredients except parmesan and mozzarella cheese into the instant pot and stir to combine.
2. Seal pot with lid and select manual high pressure for 4 minutes.

3. Release pressure using quick release method than open the lid.
4. Add parmesan and mozzarella cheese and stir well.
5. Transfer to a serving bowl and serve with chips.

Nutrition information:

Calories per serving: 382; Carbohydrates: 9.9g; Protein: 25g; Fat: 16g; Sugar: 1.4g; Sodium: 904mg; Fiber: 2g

Flavorful Salsa

(Total Time: 40 Min| Serves: 12)

Ingredients

- 12 cups tomatoes, peeled, diced, and seeded
- 4 tbsp fresh cilantro, chopped
- 3 tbsp cayenne pepper
- 2 tbsp garlic powder
- 3 tbsp sugar
- 1/2 cup vinegar
- 3 cans tomato paste

- 1 cup jalapeno peppers, chopped and seeded
- 3 large onion, chopped
- 2 green peppers, chopped
- 1 tbsp salt

Directions:

1. Add all ingredients in the instant pot and stir to combine.
2. Seal pot with lid and select manual high pressure for 30 minutes.
3. Allow to release pressure naturally then open the lid.
4. Serve and enjoy.

Nutrition information:

Calories per serving: 111; Carbohydrates: 24.7g; Protein:4.5 g; Fat: 1g; Sugar: 15.7g; Sodium: 780mg; Fiber: 5.8g

Tasty Jalapeno Cilantro Hummus
(Total Time: 35 Min| Serves: 8)

Ingredients

- 1/2 cup olive oil
- 1 tsp onion, chopped
- 1 tsp cumin
- 1/4 cup jalapeno pepper, remove seeds
- 1/2 cup fresh cilantro, chopped
- 1 tbsp tahini
- 1 cup dry garbanzo beans, soaked overnight, rinsed and drained
- 1/2 tsp sea salt

Directions:

1. Add soaked garbanzo beans and water in the instant pot.
2. Seal pot with lid and select manual and set timer for 25 minutes.
3. Allow to release pressure naturally then open the lid.
4. Drain all water from cooked garbanzo beans.
5. Add cooked garbanzo beans into the blender along with remaining ingredients and blend until smooth.

6. Pour into the serving bowl and serve with tortilla chips.

Nutrition information:

Calories per serving: 212; Carbohydrates: 15.9g; Protein:5.3 g; Fat: 15.2g; Sugar: 2.8g; Sodium: 126mg; Fiber: 4.7g

Perfect Black Bean Dip

(Total Time: 40 Min| Serves: 24)

Ingredients

- 1 1/2 cups dried black beans, rinsed
- 1/2 tsp ground coriander
- 1/2 tsp chili powder
- 1 tsp paprika
- 2 tsp ground cumin
- 1 lime juice
- 1 1/2 tbsp olive oil
- 1 3/4 cup vegetable broth

- 14.5 oz can tomatoes, diced
- 2 jalapeno peppers, chopped
- 4 garlic cloves, minced
- 1 onion, diced
- 3/4 tsp sea salt

Directions:

1. Add all ingredients to the instant pot and stir well.
2. Seal pot with lid and select bean setting and set timer for 30 minutes.
3. Allow to release pressure naturally for 10 minutes then release using quick release method.
4. Transfer bean mixture into the food processor and process until smooth.
5. Serve and enjoy.

Nutrition information:

Calories per serving: 60; Carbohydrates: 9.5g; Protein: 3.3g; Fat: 0.2g; Sugar: 1.2g; Sodium: 183mg; Fiber: 2.4g

Quick Instant Pot Popcorn
(Total Time: 10 Min| Serves: 4)

Ingredients

- 1/2 cup popcorn kernels
- 3 tbsp coconut oil
- 2 tbsp butter
- 1/8 tsp turmeric powder
- Salt

Directions:

1. Add butter, coconut oil, and turmeric into the instant pot and select sauté.
2. Add popcorn kernels and stir well to coat with oil.
3. Place glass lid on top and hold, popcorn will begin to pop in 3 minutes.
4. Turn off the instant pot when kernels have popped.
5. Remove lid and transfer popcorn into the serving bowl and season with salt.
6. Serve and enjoy.

Nutrition information:

Calories per serving: 219; Carbohydrates: 19.4g; Protein: 2.7g; Fat: 17g; Sugar: 0g; Sodium: 80mg; Fiber: 4g

Garlicky Hummus
(Total Time: 55 Min| Serves: 10)

Ingredients

- 3 garlic cloves, minced
- 1/2 cup lemon juice
- 2 tbsp olive oil
- 1/2 cup tahini
- 6 cups water
- 1 1/2 cups dry garbanzo beans, rinsed
- 1 tsp salt

Directions:

1. Add water, garbanzo beans, and salt into the instant pot.
2. Seal pot with lid and select manual high pressure for 40 minutes.
3. Allow to release pressure naturally then open the lid.
4. Drain cooked garbanzo beans in a colander over a bowl and reserve the water from cooked beans.
5. Add cooked beans, garlic, salt, lemon juice, olive oil, and tahini to a food processor.

8

6. Add 1 cup reserved cooked beans water and blend until smooth.

7. Serve and enjoy.

Nutrition information:

Calories per serving: 209; Carbohydrates: 21.3g;

Protein: 8g; Fat: 11.2g; Sugar: 3.5g; Sodium: 260mg;

Fiber: 6.4g

Delicious Onion Dip

(Total Time: 45 Min| Serves: 10)

Ingredients

- 1 tbsp soy sauce
- 8 oz cream cheese
- 12 oz sour cream
- 1/2 tsp black pepper
- 1/2 tsp baking soda
- 6 tbsp butter
- 3 large onions, peeled and sliced

- 1 tsp salt

Directions:

1. Add butter to the instant pot and select sauté.

2. Once butter is melted then add sliced onions, pepper, baking soda, and salt. Stir well and cook for 5 minutes.

3. Seal pot with lid and select manual high pressure for 16 minutes.

4. Release pressure using quick release method than open the lid carefully.

5. Set instant pot on sauté mode and stir constantly for 5 minutes or until all liquid has evaporated.

6. Transfer onion mixture to the mixing bowl.

7. Add remaining ingredients to the onion mixture and mix well. Place in refrigerator for overnight.

8. Serve chilled and enjoy.

Nutrition information:

Calories per serving: 232; Carbohydrates: 6.5g; Protein: 3.5g; Fat: 13.8g; Sugar: 2.1g; Sodium: 522mg; Fiber: 1g

Easy Spinach Dip
(Total Time: 15 Min| Serves: 15)

Ingredients

- 10 oz frozen spinach
- 4 garlic cloves, minced
- 12 oz parmesan cheese, shredded
- 12 oz Monterey jack cheese, shredded
- 1/2 cup vegetable broth
- 1/2 cup onion, chopped
- 1 cup sour cream
- 8 oz cream cheese
- 1/4 tsp pepper
- 1/2 tsp salt

Directions:

1. Add all ingredients except parmesan and Monterey jack cheese into the instant pot and stir well.
2. Seal pot with lid and select manual high pressure for 4 minutes.
3. Release pressure using quick release method than open the lid carefully.

4. Add parmesan and Monterey jack cheese and stir to combine.
5. Serve with chips.

Nutrition information:

Calories per serving: 252; Carbohydrates: 3.4g; Protein: 15.3g; Fat: 20.3g; Sugar: 0.4g; Sodium: 503mg; Fiber: 0.5g

Spicy Mexican Bean Dip
(Total Time: 55 Min| Serves: 6)

Ingredients
- 1 cup dry pinto beans, rinsed
- 1 1/2 tsp chili powder
- 4 dried red chili, stem removed
- 4 cups water
- 1 tsp salt

Directions:
1. Add beans, water, and chilies into the instant pot.

2. Seal pot with lid and select manual high pressure for 45 minutes.

3. Allow to release pressure naturally for 10 minutes then release using quick release method.

4. Transfer contents of instant pot into the blender along with chili powder and salt and blend until smooth.

5. Pour into the serving bowl and serve with tortilla chips.

Nutrition information:

Calories per serving: 115; Carbohydrates: 20.7g; Protein: 7g; Fat: 0.5g; Sugar: 0.9g; Sodium: 403mg; Fiber: 5.3g

Easy Cheesy Mexican Corn Dip

(Total Time: 20 Min| Serves: 4)

Ingredients

- 4 ears corn
- 1 cup water
- 1/4 cup basil, minced

- 1/4 cup cilantro, minced
- 1 tbsp lime juice
- 1/2 tsp black pepper
- 1/4 tsp cayenne
- 1/2 tsp cumin
- 1/2 tsp garlic powder
- 1 tsp paprika
- 1 1/2 tsp chili powder
- 1/4 cup mayonnaise
- 4 oz cream cheese
- 1 1/2 tsp salt

Directions:

1. Pour water into the instant pot then place trivet into the pot.
2. Place corn on a trivet. Seal pot with lid and select manual high pressure for 5 minutes.
3. Release pressure using quick release method than open the lid.
4. Remove corn and drain water from the pot. Cut corn from the cob.

5. Add corn kernels. Cayenne, cumin, garlic, paprika, chili powder, mayonnaise, cream cheese, pepper, and salt into the instant pot.
6. Seal pot with lid and select manual high pressure for 5 minutes.
7. Release pressure using quick release method than open the lid carefully.
8. Add basil, cilantro, and lime juice and stir well.
9. Serve with tortilla chips and enjoy.

Nutrition information:

Calories per serving: 297; Carbohydrates: 34.8g;

Protein:7.7 g; Fat: 7.3g; Sugar: 6.2g; Sodium: 1096mg;

Fiber: 5g

BREAKFAST RECIPES

Vanilla Steel Cut Oatmeal

(Total Time: 20 Min| Serves: 6)

Ingredients

- 1 cup steel cut oats
- 1 tsp cocoa powder
- 2 tsp vanilla extract
- 3 tbsp sugar
- 1 cup almond milk
- 2 1/2 cup water
- 1/4 tsp salt

Directions:

1. Add oats, sugar, almond milk, water, and salt into the instant pot and stir well.
2. Seal pot with lid and cook on manual high pressure for 10 minutes.
3. Allow to release pressure naturally for 10 minutes then release using quick release method. Open the lid carefully.
4. Add cocoa powder and vanilla extract and stir well.
5. Serve and enjoy.

Nutrition information:

Calories per serving: 171; Carbohydrates: 17.8g; Protein: 2.8 g; Fat: 8.6g; Sugar: 7.7g; Sodium: 107mg; Fiber: 2.4g

Blueberry Quinoa Breakfast
(Total Time: 15 Min| Serves: 4)

Ingredients

- 1 1/2 cups quinoa, rinsed and drained
- 1/4 cup pistachios, chopped
- 1 cup plain yogurt
- 1 cup apple juice
- 3/4 cup apple, grated
- 1 tbsp honey
- 1/4 cup raisins
- 1 cinnamon stick
- 1 1/2 cups water
- 1/2 cup blueberries

Directions:

1. Add water, quinoa, and cinnamon stick into the instant pot.
2. Seal pot with lid and select manual and set timer for 1 minute.
3. Allow to release pressure naturally for 10 minutes then release using quick release method. Open the lid carefully.
4. Discard cinnamon stick from quinoa and transfer quinoa to the mixing bowl.
5. Add raisins, apple juice, apple, and honey into the bowl and stir to combine. Place quinoa bowl in refrigerator for 1 hour.
6. Add yogurt to quinoa and stir well.
7. Top with blueberries and pistachios.
8. Serve and enjoy.

Nutrition information:

Calories per serving: 402; Carbohydrates: 73.1g; Protein: 13.8g; Fat: 1.3g; Sugar: 26.4g; Sodium: 73mg; Fiber: 6.8g

Healthy Breakfast Porridge

(Total Time: 10 Min| Serves: 2)

Ingredients

- 1 tbsp honey
- 2 tsp coconut oil, melted
- 1 cup water
- 1/2 cup shredded coconut
- 1/2 cup pecan halves
- 1/4 cup pepitas, shelled
- 1/2 cup cashews

Directions:

1. Add shredded coconut, pecan halves, pepitas, and cashews into the food processor and process for 30 seconds.
2. Transfer contents to the instant pot and stir in honey, water, and melted oil.
3. Seal pot with lid and select porridge and set timer for 3 minutes.
4. Release pressure using quick release method than open the lid.
5. Stir well and serve.

Nutrition information:

Calories per serving: 758; Carbohydrates: 30.9g;
Protein: 12g; Fat: 71.1g; Sugar: 13.6g; Sodium: 13mg;
Fiber: 8.9g

Apple Steel Cut Oatmeal
(Total Time: 20 Min| Serves: 2)

Ingredients

- 1 cup steel cut oats
- 1/4 cup raisins
- 1/4 cup brown sugar
- 2 1/2 cups water
- 1/2 tsp cinnamon
- 1 tsp vanilla
- 2 apples, chopped
- 1 tbsp butter

Directions:

1. Add butter to the instant pot and select sauté.
2. Add oats to the melted butter and stir for 3 minutes.

3. Add apples, water, cinnamon, and vanilla. Stir well.
4. Seal pot with lid and select manual high pressure for 10 minutes.
5. Release pressure using quick release method than open the lid.
6. Add raisins and brown sugar and stir well.
7. Serve and enjoy.

Nutrition information:

Calories per serving: 453; Carbohydrates: 91.4g; Protein: 6.6g; Fat: 8.9g; Sugar: 52.2g; Sodium: 62mg; Fiber: 10.5g

Creamy Maple Oats

(Total Time: 20 Min| Serves: 4)

Ingredients

- 1 cup steel cut oats
- 1/4 tsp cinnamon
- 1 tbsp brown sugar

- 2 tbsp maple syrup
- 1/4 cup pumpkin
- 1 tsp vanilla
- 1 1/2 cups water
- 14 oz can coconut milk
- 1/2 tsp salt

Directions:

1. Add oats, vanilla, water, coconut milk, and salt into the instant pot and stir well.
2. Seal pot with lid and select manual and set timer for 10 minutes.
3. Allow to release pressure naturally then open the lid.
4. Add brown sugar, cinnamon, maple syrup, and pumpkin and stir well.
5. Serve and enjoy.

Nutrition information:

Calories per serving: 316; Carbohydrates: 27g; Protein: 4.9g; Fat: 19g; Sugar: 9g; Sodium: 310mg; Fiber: 2.6g

Perfect Quinoa Breakfast Bowls

(Total Time: 25 Min| Serves: 6)

Ingredients

- 1 1/2 cups quinoa, soaked in water for 1 hour
- 2 tsp vanilla extract
- 1/4 cup maple syrup
- 1 tsp ground cinnamon
- 1 1/2 cups water
- 15 oz can almond milk
- 1/4 tsp salt

Directions:

1. Drain soaked quinoa and rinsed well.
2. Add quinoa to the instant pot along with almond milk, vanilla, maple syrup, cinnamon, water, and salt. Stir well.
3. Seal pot with lid and select manual high pressure for 1 minute.
4. Allow to release pressure naturally then open the lid.
5. Divide quinoa into the six serving bowls and place in refrigerator until ready to serve.

23

6. When serving, top with fresh fruit, non-dairy milk, and shredded coconut and any other your choice toppings.

Nutrition information:

Calories per serving: 359; Carbohydrates: 40.5g; Protein: 7.6g; Fat: 19.5g; Sugar: 10.4g; Sodium: 113mg; Fiber: 4.7g

Gluten Free Buckwheat Porridge

(Total Time: 30 Min| Serves: 4)

Ingredients

- 1 cup buckwheat groats, rinsed
- 1/2 tsp vanilla extract
- 1 tsp cinnamon
- 1/4 cup raisins
- 1 medium banana, sliced
- 3 cups almond milk
- 1/4 cup nuts, chopped

Directions:

1. Add buckwheat to the instant pot.
2. Add almond milk, vanilla, cinnamon, raisins, and banana. Stir well.
3. Seal pot with lid and select manual high pressure for 6 minutes.
4. Allow to release pressure naturally then open the lid.
5. Stir well and divide into serving bowls.
6. Top with chopped nuts and serve.

Nutrition information:

Calories per serving: 622; Carbohydrates: 47.8g; Protein: 10g; Fat: 48.4g; Sugar: 16.2g; Sodium: 89mg; Fiber: 9.2g

Easy Brown Rice Pudding

(Total Time: 45 Min| Serves: 4)

Ingredients

- 1 cup brown rice, rinsed
- 1/2 cup heavy cream

- 3 tbsp honey
- 1/2 cup raisins
- 1 tbsp butter
- 1 cinnamon stick
- 1 tbsp vanilla
- 1 1/2 cups water

Directions:

1. Add brown rice, butter, cinnamon stick, vanilla, and water into the instant pot and stir well.
2. Seal pot with lid and select manual and set timer for 20 minutes.
3. Allow to release pressure naturally then open the lid.
4. Discard cinnamon stick. Add heavy cream, honey, and raisins and stir well.
5. Set instant pot on sauté mode and simmer for 5 minutes.
6. Stir well and serve.

Nutrition information:

Calories per serving: 361; Carbohydrates: 64.4g; Protein: 4.5g; Fat: 9.8g; Sugar: 24.1g; Sodium: 34mg; Fiber: 2.3g

Chocó Cherry Oats

(Total Time: 25 Min| Serves: 4)

Ingredients

- 1/2 cup steel cut oats
- 1/4 tsp cinnamon
- 1 tsp cocoa powder
- 2 tbsp honey
- 12 frozen cherries, pitted
- 1 1/2 cups water
- 1/4 tsp salt

Directions:

1. Add all ingredients to the instant pot and stir well.
2. Seal pot with lid and select manual and set timer for 10 minutes.
3. Allow to release pressure naturally for 10 minutes then release using quick release method.
4. Stir well and serve.

Nutrition information:

Calories per serving: 102; Carbohydrates: 22g; Protein: 1.5g; Fat: 0.7g; Sugar: 14.8g; Sodium: 166mg; Fiber: 1.3g

Healthy Butternut Squash Porridge

(Total Time: 30 Min| Serves: 6)

Ingredients

- 1 cup butternut squash, shredded
- 1 cup rice, soaked, rinsed and drained
- 3 cups coconut milk
- 1/2 tsp cinnamon
- 3 tbsp brown sugar
- 1/2 cup raisins
- 2 tbsp butter
- 1/4 tsp salt

Directions:

1. Add butter to the instant pot and select sauté.
2. Add rice in melted butter and stir to coat.
3. Add remaining ingredients and stir well to combine.
4. Seal pot with lid and select manual high pressure for 6 minutes.
5. Allow to release pressure naturally then open the lid.
6. Stir well and serve.

Nutrition information:

Calories per serving: 487; Carbohydrates: 48.2g; Protein: 5.6g; Fat: 32.7g; Sugar: 16.1g; Sodium: 147mg; Fiber: 4.1g

MAIN DISHES

Quick Mac and Cheese
(Total Time: 15 Min| Serves: 8)

Ingredients

- 16 oz pasta
- 2 cup cheddar cheese, shredded
- 1 tsp Dijon mustard
- 3/4 cup coconut milk
- 3 tbsp butter
- 4 1/2 cups water

Directions:

1. Add pasta, butter, and water into the instant pot. Stir well.
2. Seal pot with lid and select manual and set timer for 4 minutes.
3. Release pressure using quick release method than open the lid.
4. Add cheese, mustard, and coconut milk and stir well to combine.
5. Serve and enjoy.

Nutrition information:

Calories per serving: 368; Carbohydrates: 32.7g; Protein: 14g; Fat: 20.4g; Sugar: 0.9g; Sodium: 253mg; Fiber: 0.5g

Thai Chickpea Curry

(Total Time: 30 Min| Serves: 5)

Ingredients

- 15 oz can chickpeas
- 1/2 cup water
- 1 cup brown lentils, rinsed and drained
- 14 oz coconut milk
- 12 cherry tomatoes, diced
- 2 tbsp curry paste
- 3 garlic cloves, minced
- 2 tbsp ginger, grated
- 3 green onions, chopped
- 1 tbsp olive oil
- 1/2 tsp salt

Directions:

1. Add oil into the instant pot and select sauté.
2. Add garlic, ginger, and green onions and sauté for minutes.
3. Add water, chickpeas, lentils, coconut milk, and salt and stir well.
4. Seal pot with lid and select manual high pressure for 15 minutes.
5. Allow to release pressure naturally then open the lid.
6. Stir well and serve over rice.

Nutrition information:

Calories per serving: 534; Carbohydrates: 61.2g; Protein: 18.2g; Fat: 26.9g; Sugar: 12.3g; Sodium: 528mg; Fiber: 15.2g

Delicious Lentil Chili

(Total Time: 30 Min| Serves: 6)

Ingredients

- 16 oz dry lentils, rinsed
- 1/4 cup cilantro, chopped
- 15 oz can tomatoes, diced
- 4 tsp chili powder
- 4 garlic cloves, chopped
- 6 cups vegetable broth
- 1 bell pepper, chopped
- 1 tbsp olive oil
- 1 onion, chopped

Directions:

1. Add olive oil into the instant pot and select sauté.
2. Add bell pepper and onion into the hot oil and sauté for 5 minutes.
3. Add garlic and chili powder and sauté for 1 minute.
4. Add remaining ingredients and stir well.
5. Seal pot with lid and select manual and set timer for 15 minutes.
6. Allow to release pressure naturally then open the lid.
7. Stir well and serve.

Nutrition information:

Calories per serving: 363; Carbohydrates: 54.8g;

Protein: 25.7g; Fat: 4.9g; Sugar: 6.6g; Sodium: 938mg;

Fiber: 25.6g

Flavorful Mexican Rice

(Total Time: 30 Min| Serves: 4)

Ingredients

- 2 cups brown rice, rinsed and drained
- 2 cups water
- 2 cups vegetable broth
- 1/2 cup tomato sauce
- 1/2 tsp cumin powder
- 3 garlic cloves, minced
- 1/4 cup onion, chopped
- 2 tbsp olive oil
- 1/2 tsp salt

Directions:

1. Add olive oil into the instant pot and select sauté.
2. Add garlic, onion, and cumin and sauté for 2 minutes.
3. Add rice and stir for 4 minutes.
4. Add tomato sauce and stir well to coat.
5. Add broth, water, and salt and stir well.
6. Seal pot with lid and select manual and set timer for 22 minutes.
7. Allow to release pressure naturally then open the lid.
8. Stir well and serve.

Nutrition information:

Calories per serving: 438; Carbohydrates: 76g; Protein: 10.2g; Fat: 10.4g; Sugar: 2g; Sodium: 841mg; Fiber: 3.9g

Garlic Onion Rice Pilaf
(Total Time: 30 Min| Serves: 6)

Ingredients

- 1 1/2 cups rice, rinsed
- 3 garlic cloves, minced
- 1/2 cup onion, diced
- 2 tbsp butter
- 1/4 cup fresh parsley, chopped
- 1 3/4 cups vegetable broth
- 1/2 tsp salt

Directions:

1. Add butter to the instant pot and select sauté.
2. Add onion, garlic, and salt in melted butter and sauté for 2 minutes.
3. Add rice and stir to coat. Add broth and stir well.
4. Seal pot with lid and select manual high pressure for 22 minutes.
5. Allow to release pressure naturally then open the lid.
6. Fluff the rice using a fork. Add parsley and stir well.

7. Serve and enjoy.

Nutrition information:

Calories per serving: 221; Carbohydrates: 38.7g; Protein: 5g; Fat: 4.6g; Sugar: 0.7g; Sodium: 448mg; Fiber: 0.9g

Delicious Potato Risotto

(Total Time: 25 Min| Serves: 4)

Ingredients

- 2 cups rice, uncooked
- 4 tbsp white wine
- 1 onion, chopped
- 1 tbsp olive oil
- 1 tbsp tomato paste
- 4 cups vegetable stock
- 1 large potato, cubed
- 1 tsp salt

Directions:

1. Add oil to the instant pot and select sauté.

2. Add onion in hot oil and sauté for 4 minutes.

3. Add rice and stir for 2 minutes.

4. Add white wine and stir until the rice absorbs the wine.

5. Add stock, potatoes, tomato paste, and salt. Stir well.

6. Seal pot with lid and select manual high pressure for 5 minutes.

7. Allow to release pressure naturally then open the lid.

8. Serve and enjoy.

Nutrition information:

Calories per serving: 468; Carbohydrates: 94.3g; Protein: 8.9g; Fat: 4.7g; Sugar: 3.1g; Sodium: 777mg; Fiber: 4g

Simple Parsnip Gratin
(Total Time: 20 Min| Serves: 5)

Ingredients

- 5 cups parsnip, sliced
- 1 tbsp pepper
- 2 cups vegetable broth
- 3 garlic cloves, minced
- 3 tbsp olive oil
- 2 cups mozzarella cheese
- 1 cup cream cheese
- 1 tbsp garlic powder

Directions:

1. Add all ingredients except cheese into the instant pot.
2. Seal pot with lid and select manual high pressure for 4 minutes.
3. Allow to release pressure naturally then open the lid.
4. Set the instant pot on sauté mode. Sprinkle mozzarella cheese on top and cook for 5 minutes.
5. Serve and enjoy.

Nutrition information:

Calories per serving: 393; Carbohydrates: 28.6g;
Protein: 10.8g; Fat: 27.6g; Sugar: 7.2g; Sodium: 525mg;
Fiber: 7.1g

Mushroom Risotto

(Total Time: 30 Min| Serves: 6)

Ingredients

- 2 cup Arborio rice
- 2 tbsp olive oil
- 2 tbsp butter
- 1 onion, diced
- 4 cups vegetable stock
- 1 1/2 cups parmesan cheese, grated
- 2 garlic cloves, minced
- 8 oz portabella mushrooms, sliced

Directions:

1. Add olive oil and 1 tbsp Butter into the instant pot and select sauté.
2. Add garlic and onion and sauté until softened.
3. Add rice and mushrooms and stir to coat. Stir in vegetable stock.
4. Seal the pot with lid and select manual high pressure for 8 minutes.
5. Release the pressure using quick release method than open the lid.
6. Add remaining 1 tbsp butter and parmesan cheese and stir well.
7. Serve and enjoy.

Nutrition information:

Calories per serving: 477; Carbohydrates: 55.7g; Protein: 17.5g; Fat: 19.3g; Sugar: 2.8g; Sodium: 995mg; Fiber: 2.7g

Veggie Pasta

(Total Time: 30 Min| Serves: 4)

Ingredients

- 1/2 lb pasta
- 2 medium carrots, peeled and chopped
- 1/4 green onion, sliced
- 1/4 tsp red chili flakes
- 1 tsp ground ginger
- 3 garlic cloves, minced
- 2 cups baby spinach, chopped
- 1 cup frozen peas
- 8 oz mushrooms, sliced
- 1/4 cup coconut amino
- 2 cups vegetable broth
- 1/4 tsp pepper
- 1 tsp salt

Directions:

1. Add all ingredients except spinach in instant pot and stir to combine.
2. Seal pot with lid and select manual high pressure for 4 minutes.

3. Allow to release pressure naturally then open the lid.
4. Add spinach and stir, let sit for 5 minutes.
5. Serve and enjoy.

Nutrition information:

Calories per serving: 262; Carbohydrates: 46.8g;

Protein: 13.6g; Fat: 2.4g; Sugar: 4.8g; Sodium: 1207mg;

Fiber: 4g

Healthy Veggie Gumbo

(Total Time: 20 Min| Serves: 4)

Ingredients

- 1 cup red kidney beans, soaked overnight in water
- 1 bell pepper, chopped
- 2 tbsp olive oil
- 3 garlic cloves, chopped
- 1 cup mushrooms, sliced
- 2 cups vegetable stock

- 2 tbsp tamari sauce
- 2 medium zucchini, sliced

Directions:

1. Add all ingredients into the instant pot and stir well.
2. Seal pot with lid and select manual high pressure for 8 minutes,
3. Allow to release pressure naturally then open the lid.
4. Stir well and serve.

Nutrition information:

Calories per serving: 255; Carbohydrates: 36g; Protein: 13.5g; Fat: 1.6g; Sugar: 5.1g; Sodium: 700mg; Fiber: 8.8g

SIDE DISHES

Rosemary Garlic Potatoes

(Total Time: 10 Min| Serves: 4)

Ingredients

- 1 lb potatoes, scrubbed and sliced
- 2 garlic cloves, sliced
- 1/4 tsp rosemary, dried
- 1 tbsp olive oil
- Salt

Directions

1. Pour 1 cup water into the instant pot and place steamer basket into the pot.
2. Add sliced potatoes to the steamer basket.
3. Seal pot with lid and select manual high pressure for 4 minutes.
4. Release pressure using quick release method than open the lid.
5. Add olive oil, garlic, and rosemary into the oven-safe dish and microwave for 1 minute.
6. Add sliced potatoes into the dish and stir to coat.
7. Serve and enjoy.

Nutrition information:

Calories per serving: 111; Carbohydrates: 18.4g; Protein: 2g; Fat: 0.5g; Sugar: 1.3g; Sodium: 46mg; Fiber: 2.8g

Cauliflower Mashed
(Total Time: 15 Min| Serves: 4)

Ingredients:
- 1 large cauliflower head, cut into florets
- 1 tbsp butter
- 1 cup water
- 1/4 tsp garlic powder
- 1/4 tsp salt

Directions
1. Pour water into the instant pot then place steamer basket in the pot.
2. Place cauliflower florets into the steamer basket.
3. Seal pot with lid and select manual high pressure for 5 minutes.
4. Release pressure using quick release method than open the lid carefully.

5. Drain cauliflower florets well and place in large bowl.
6. Add butter, garlic powder, pepper, and salt and mash until smooth and creamy.
7. Serve and enjoy.

Nutrition information:

Calories per serving: 79; Carbohydrates: 11.3g; Protein: 4.2g; Fat: 3.1g; Sugar: 5.1g; Sodium: 233mg; Fiber: 5.3g

Roasted Potatoes

(Total Time: 20 Min| Serves: 4)

Ingredients

- 1 1/2 lbs russet potatoes cut into wedges
- 1/4 cup olive oil
- 1 cup vegetable stock
- 1 tsp garlic powder
- 1/2 tsp onion powder
- 1/4 tsp black pepper
- 1/4 tsp paprika
- 1 tsp sea salt

Directions:

1. Add olive oil to the instant pot and select sauté.
2. Add potatoes to the hot oil and sauté for 8 minutes.
3. Add onion powder, garlic powder, paprika, vegetable stock, pepper, and salt. Mix well.
4. Seal pot with lid and select manual low pressure for 7 minutes.
5. Release pressure using quick release method the open the lid.
6. Serve and enjoy.

Nutrition information:

Calories per serving: 232; Carbohydrates: 28.1g; Protein: 3g; Fat: 13.3g; Sugar: 2.8g; Sodium: 659mg; Fiber: 4.3g

Apple Squash Mash

(Total Time: 20 Min| Serves: 4)

Ingredients

- 1 lb butternut squash, cut into 2" pieces
- 2 apples, cored and sliced

- 1 onion, sliced
- 1/4 tsp ground cinnamon
- 1/8 tsp ginger powder
- 1 cup water
- 2 tbsp coconut oil
- 1/4 tsp salt

Directions:

1. Pour water into the instant pot and place steamer basket into the pot.
2. Toss apples, butternut squash, and onion together and put in a steamer basket. Season with salt.
3. Seal pot with lid and select manual and set timer for 8 minutes.
4. Release pressure using quick release method than open the lid.
5. Transfer apple and squash mixture into the mixing bowl and mash until smooth.
6. Add coconut oil, ginger, and cinnamon and mix well to combine.
7. Serve warm and enjoy.

Nutrition information:

Calories per serving: 179; Carbohydrates: 31.4g; Protein: 1.8g; Fat: 7.1g; Sugar: 15.3g; Sodium: 156mg; Fiber: 5.6g

Cheese Asparagus

(Total Time: 15 Min| Serves: 2)

Ingredients

- 1 bunch asparagus, ends trimmed and cut into pieces
- 3 tbsp parmesan cheese, grated
- 3 garlic cloves, minced
- 3 tbsp butter
- 1 cup water

Directions:

1. Pour water into the instant pot then place trivet into the pot.
2. Place asparagus on aluminum foil square with garlic and butter then curve the edges of foil.
3. Place foil on a trivet. Seal pot with lid and select manual high pressure for 8 minutes.
4. Release pressure using quick release method than open the lid.
5. Sprinkle with parmesan cheese and serve.

Nutrition information:

Calories per serving: 232; Carbohydrates: 4.6g; Protein: 6.7g; Fat: 13.2g; Sugar: 1.6g; Sodium: 309mg; Fiber: 1.8g

Buttery Green Beans
(Total Time: 15 Min| Serves: 4)

Ingredients

- 1 lb green beans
- 2 tbsp butter
- 1 1/4 cup water
- 1 garlic clove, minced
- Pepper
- Salt

Directions:

1. Add all ingredients into the instant pot and stir well.
2. Seal pot with lid and select manual low pressure for 5 minutes.
3. Release pressure using quick release method than open the lid carefully.
4. Serve and enjoy.

Nutrition information:

Calories per serving: 87; Carbohydrates: 8.4g; Protein: 2.2g; Fat: 5.9g; Sugar: 1.6g; Sodium: 89mg; Fiber: 3.9g

Smooth Turnip Mash

(Total Time: 25 Min| Serves: 4)

Ingredients

- 4 medium turnips, peeled and diced
- 1/2 cup vegetable broth
- 1 onion, diced
- 1/4 cup sour cream
- Pepper
- Salt

Directions:

1. Add turnips, broth, and onion into the instant pot.
2. Seal pot with lid and select manual high pressure for 5 minutes.
3. Allow to release pressure naturally for 10 minutes then release using quick release method.
4. Drain turnip well and transfer to mixing bowl and mash turnips until smooth.
5. Add sour cream and stir well. Season with pepper and salt.
6. Serve warm and enjoy.

Nutrition information:

Calories per serving: 82; Carbohydrates: 11.3g; Protein: 2.4g; Fat: 3.2g; Sugar: 6.3g; Sodium: 223mg; Fiber: 2.6g

Easy Braised Parsnips

(Total Time: 15 Min| Serves: 4)

Ingredients

- 1 1/2 lbs parsnips, peeled and sliced
- 1/4 cup vegetable broth
- 2 tbsp maple syrup
- 3 tbsp balsamic vinegar
- 1/8 tsp pepper
- 1/2 tsp salt

Directions:

1. Add parsnips, vinegar, and broth into the instant pot.
2. Seal pot with lid and cook on high pressure for 3 minutes.
3. Release pressure using quick release method than open the lid.
4. Add maple syrup and stir well. Season with pepper and salt.
5. Serve and enjoy.

Nutrition information:

Calories per serving: 159; Carbohydrates: 37.5g; Protein: 2.4g; Fat: 0.6g; Sugar: 14.2g; Sodium: 357mg; Fiber: 8.4g

Stir Fried Mushroom

(Total Time: 30 Min| Serves: 4)

Ingredients

- 24 oz Bella mushrooms, sliced
- 1 tsp cumin seeds
- 1/4 tsp turmeric powder
- 3 curry leaves
- 1 tbsp olive oil
- 3 tbsp water
- 1/2 tsp mustard seeds
- 2 tsp salt

Directions:

1. Add olive oil to the instant pot and select sauté.
2. Add cumin seeds and mustard seeds into the hot oil and let them pop.
3. Add sliced mushrooms, turmeric, curry leaves, and salt. Stir well.
4. Add water and stir. Seal pot with lid and select steam and set timer for 2 minutes.
5. Release pressure using quick release method than open the lid.
6. Set the instant pot on sauté mode.
7. Stir mushroom and simmer for 3-4 minutes.
8. Serve and enjoy.

Nutrition information:

Calories per serving: 83; Carbohydrates: 5.3g; Protein: 5.1g; Fat: 3.8g; Sugar: 0g; Sodium: 1164mg; Fiber: 0.2g

Flavorful Butternut Squash
(Total Time: 13 Min| Serves: 4)

Ingredients

- 2 lbs butternut squash, chopped
- 1 tbsp pumpkin pie spice
- 1 tsp dried oregano
- 1 onion, chopped
- 3/4 cup water
- 1 tsp garlic powder
- 1 tsp chili powder

Directions:

1. Add all ingredients to the instant pot and stir well.
2. Seal pot with lid and select manual high pressure for 3 minutes.
3. Release pressure using quick release method than open the lid.
4. Stir and serve.

Nutrition information:

Calories per serving: 123; Carbohydrates: 31.2g; Protein: 2.9g; Fat: 0.6g; Sugar: 6.5g; Sodium: 19mg; Fiber: 5.8g

SOUP & STEW RECIPES

Delicious Turmeric Spinach Lentil Soup
(Total Time: 30 Min| Serves: 6)

Ingredients
- 1 cup red lentils, rinsed
- 1 tbsp lemon juice
- 4 cups fresh spinach, chopped
- 1 tbsp turmeric
- 2 tsp cumin
- 2 cups vegetable broth
- 1 1/2 cups tomatoes, diced
- 2 cans coconut milk
- 1 tbsp ginger, minced
- 3 garlic cloves, minced
- 3 celery stalks, chopped
- 2 carrots, peeled and chopped
- 3 onions, chopped
- 2 tbsp olive oil
- 1/2 tsp salt

Directions:

1. Add all ingredients into the instant pot except lemon juice and spinach. Stir well.
2. Seal pot with lid and select manual high pressure for 15 minutes.
3. Release pressure using quick release method than open the lid.
4. Add lemon juice and spinach and stir well.
5. Serve and enjoy.

Nutrition information:

Calories per serving: 264; Carbohydrates: 32.6g; Protein: 12.6g; Fat: 4.3g; Sugar: 5.7g; Sodium: 503mg; Fiber: 13g

Flavorful Coconut Lentil Soup

(Total Time: 25 Min| Serves: 4)

Ingredients

- 14 oz can coconut milk
- 14 oz can tomatoes, crushed
- 3/4 cup dry red split lentils, rinsed
- 1/4 tsp red pepper flakes
- 1 tbsp curry powder
- 1 tbsp ginger paste

- 2 garlic cloves, minced
- 1 medium onion, diced
- Pepper
- Salt

Directions:

1. Add all ingredients into the instant pot and stir well.
2. Seal pot with lid and select manual high pressure for 15 minutes.
3. Release pressure using quick release method than open the lid carefully.
4. Stir well and serve.

Nutrition information:

Calories per serving: 580; Carbohydrates: 35.9g; Protein: 14.1g; Fat: 34.9g; Sugar: 5.4g; Sodium: 351mg; Fiber: 6.8g

Carrot Split Pea Soup

(Total Time: 30 Min| Serves: 4)

Ingredients

- 1/2 tbsp lemon juice
- 2 tbsp olive oil
- 4 carrots, peeled and chopped
- 2 large onion, chopped
- 5 cups water
- 1 lb dry split peas, rinsed and drained
- 1 tsp salt

Directions:

1. Add olive oil into the instant pot and select sauté.
2. Add onion and carrots in hot oil and sauté until softened.
3. Add split peas and 5 cups water into the instant pot and stir well.
4. Seal pot with lid and select manual high pressure for 15 minutes.
5. Allow to release pressure naturally for 10 minutes then release using quick release method.
6. Add lemon juice and salt and stir well to combine.
7. Serve and enjoy.

Nutrition information:

Calories per serving: 502; Carbohydrates: 81.5g; Protein: 29.2 g; Fat: 1.2g; Sugar: 15.3g; Sodium: 653mg; Fiber: 32g

Creamy Broccoli Soup

(Total Time: 30 Min| Serves: 4)

Ingredients

- 1 lb broccoli, chopped
- 1 tbsp hot sauce
- 16 oz half and half
- 3 cups vegetable broth
- 8 oz cheddar cheese, shredded
- 1 small onion, diced
- 2 medium carrots, shredded
- 1/2 tsp salt

Directions:

1. Add broccoli, carrot, onion, vegetable broth, and salt into the instant pot and stir well.
2. Seal pot with lid and select manual high pressure for 15 minutes.

3. Release pressure using quick release method than open the lid.
4. Set the instant pot on sauté mode. Add remaining ingredients into the instant pot and stir continuously for 3 minutes.
5. Turn off the instant pot and using immersion blender puree the soup until smooth and creamy.
6. Stir well and serve.

Nutrition information:

Calories per serving: 463; Carbohydrates: 18.5g; Protein: 24.8 g; Fat: 20.4g; Sugar: 5.2g; Sodium: 1416mg; Fiber: 4.1g

Perfect Corn Soup

(Total Time: 25 Min| Serves: 4)

Ingredients

- 2 1/2 cups corn kernels
- 1 1/2 tsp ground cumin
- 2 tsp ginger, grated
- 2 tsp garlic, minced

- 2 tsp olive oil
- 1 tbsp soy sauce
- 1 cup cabbage, minced
- 1 cup carrot, minced
- 5 cups vegetable broth
- Pepper
- Salt

Directions:

1. Add all ingredients into the instant pot and stir well.
2. Seal pot with lid and select manual high pressure for 10 minutes.
3. Allow to release pressure naturally then open the lid.
4. Remove 3 cups of soup from instant pot and puree using a blender until smooth.
5. Return blended soup into the instant pot and stir well.
6. Season with pepper and salt.
7. Serve and enjoy.

Nutrition information:

Calories per serving: 177; Carbohydrates: 24.8g; Protein: 10.2g; Fat: 5.4g; Sugar: 6g; Sodium: 1257mg; Fiber: 4g

Creamy Mushroom Soup
(Total Time: 35 Min| Serves: 4)

Ingredients

- 2/3 cup coconut milk
- 3 cups vegetable broth
- 1 tsp dried thyme
- 16 oz crimini mushrooms, sliced
- 4 garlic cloves, minced
- 1 large carrot, peeled and chopped
- 1 large celery stalk, chopped
- 1 medium onion, chopped
- 2 tsp olive oil
- 1/2 tsp ground pepper
- 1/2 tsp salt

Directions:

1. Add olive oil into the instant pot and select sauté.
2. Add onion, carrot, and celery into the hot oil and sauté for 3-4 minutes.
3. Add mushrooms, thyme, garlic, and pepper and sauté for 2-3 minutes.
4. Add broth and salt and stir well.
5. Seal pot with lid and select manual high pressure for 10 minutes.
6. Release pressure using quick release method than open the lid.
7. Transfer soup into the blender along with coconut milk and blend until smooth and creamy.
8. Serve and enjoy.

Nutrition information:

Calories per serving: 197; Carbohydrates: 13.5g; Protein: 8.2g; Fat: 13.1g; Sugar: 6g; Sodium: 898mg; Fiber: 3g

Cauliflower Squash Soup
(Total Time: 30 Min| Serves: 6)

Ingredients

- 1 cauliflower head, chopped
- 1 butternut squash, peeled and cubed
- 1/4 tsp nutmeg
- 1/2 tsp lemon zest
- 1/2 tsp sage
- 1 cup water
- 4 cups vegetable broth
- 2 garlic cloves, minced
- 1 onion, chopped
- 1 tbsp olive oil
- 2 carrots, peeled and chopped
- 1 apple, peeled and chopped
- 1/2 tsp pepper
- 1/2 tsp salt

Directions:

1. Add oil into the instant pot and select sauté.
2. Add onion into the hot oil and sauté for 3 minutes.
3. Add garlic and saute for 1 minute.
4. Add cauliflower, carrots, apple, and squash and stir well to combine.

5. Add lemon zest, sage, nutmeg, pepper, and salt. Stir.

6. Add water and vegetable broth and stir.

7. Seal pot with lid and select soup setting and set timer for 15 minutes.

8. Allow to release pressure naturally then open the lid.

9. Serve and enjoy.

Nutrition information:

Calories per serving: 101; Carbohydrates: 14.2g; Protein: 4.8g; Fat: 0.6g; Sugar: 7.6g; Sodium: 732mg; Fiber: 3.3g

Hearty Lentil Stew

(Total Time: 25 Min| Serves: 8)

Ingredients

- 1 lb dry red lentils, soaked overnight
- 2 cups vegetable broth
- 1 can coconut milk

- 1/2 tsp paprika
- 1/2 tsp turmeric
- 1 tbsp curry powder
- 14.5 oz can tomatoes, diced
- 1 tbsp garlic, minced
- 1 small onion, diced
- 2 tbsp olive oil
- 1/4 tsp black pepper
- 1/2 tsp salt

Directions:

1. Add oil into the instant pot and select sauté.
2. Add garlic and onion in hot oil and sauté for 3-4 minutes.
3. Add tomatoes and stir well.
4. Add remaining ingredients and stir well to combine.
5. Seal pot with lid and select manual high pressure for 6 minutes.
6. Release pressure using quick release method than open the lid.
7. Stir well and serve.

Nutrition information:

Calories per serving: 275; Carbohydrates: 39.1g; Protein: 16.8g; Fat: 6.1g; Sugar: 3.5g; Sodium: 455mg; Fiber: 18.7g

Eggplant Stew
(Total Time: 35 Min| Serves: 4)

Ingredients

- 2 eggplants, cut into chunks
- 1 tsp sugar
- 1 tbsp red wine vinegar
- 2 tbsp tomato paste
- 1 1/2 cups tomatoes, chopped
- 10 olives
- 2 tbsp capers
- 1/4 cup fresh basil leaves
- 1 chili pepper, chopped
- 1 large onion, chopped
- 2 garlic cloves, minced
- 1/4 cup olive oil
- 1 tsp salt

Directions:

1. Add oil into the instant pot and select sauté.
2. Add chili pepper in hot oil and sauté for 30 seconds.
3. Add onion and eggplant and sauté for 5 minutes.
4. Add remaining ingredients and stir well to combine.
5. Seal pot with lid and select manual high pressure for 20 minutes.
6. Release pressure using quick release method than open the lid.
7. Stir well and serve.

Nutrition information:

Calories per serving: 231; Carbohydrates: 26.3g;
Protein: 4.4g; Fat: 14.6g; Sugar: 13.7g; Sodium: 823mg;
Fiber: 12.2g

Flavors African Stew

(Total Time: 25 Min| Serves: 6)

Ingredients

- 2 cups spinach, chopped
- 15 oz can chickpeas, rinsed and drained
- 1 cup coconut milk
- 1/3 cup peanut butter
- 1 tbsp curry powder
- 28 oz can tomatoes, diced
- 1 cup vegetable broth
- 2 potatoes, diced
- 2 tsp garlic, minced
- 3 celery stalks, diced
- 1 carrot, diced
- 2 onions, sliced
- 1 tsp sea salt

Directions:

1. Add all ingredients into the instant pot and stir to combine.
2. Seal pot with lid and select manual high pressure for 10 minutes.

3. Allow to release pressure naturally then open the lid.

4. Stir well and serve.

Nutrition information:

Calories per serving: 371; Carbohydrates: 45.1g; Protein: 12.2g; Fat: 18.1g; Sugar: 10.4; Sodium: 1033mg; Fiber: 10.6g

BEAN RECIPES

Delicious Vegan Black Beans
(Total Time: 60 Min| Serves: 12)

Ingredients

- 1 lb dry black beans, rinsed
- 1/2 tsp paprika
- 1/2 tsp cumin
- 1/2 tsp coriander
- 1/2 tsp garlic powder
- 5 1/2 cups water

Directions:

1. Add all ingredients into the instant pot and stir to combine.
2. Seal pot with lid and select manual high pressure for 50 minutes.
3. Allow to release pressure naturally then open the lid.
4. Stir well and serve.

Nutrition information:

Calories per serving: 130; Carbohydrates: 23.8g; Protein: 8.2 g; Fat: 0.6g; Sugar: 0.8g; Sodium: 5mg; Fiber: 5.8g

Refried Beans

(Total Time: 30 Min| Serves: 8)

Ingredients

- 16 oz pinto beans, soaked overnight in water, rinsed and drained
- 1 onion, diced
- 3 tsp cilantro, chopped
- 1 tbsp cumin
- 2 tsp cayenne
- 2 jalapeno pepper, chopped
- 16 oz vegetable broth
- 1 tsp salt

Directions:

1. Add all ingredients into the instant pot and stir well.

2. Seal pot with lid and select manual high pressure for 12 minutes.
3. Allow to release pressure naturally then open the lid.
4. Mash beans mixture using potato masher until smooth.
5. Serve and enjoy.

Nutrition information:

Calories per serving: 217; Carbohydrates: 37.8g; Protein: 13.7 g; Fat: 1.3g; Sugar: 2.1g; Sodium: 480mg; Fiber: 9.4g

Delicious Pinto Beans

(Total Time: 35 Min| Serves: 8)

Ingredients

- 1 lb dry pinto beans, soaked overnight, rinsed and drained
- 2 bay leaves
- 1 tsp ground black pepper

- 1 tsp oregano
- 1 tsp cumin
- 1 tbsp mustard
- 2 tbsp chili powder
- 8 oz can tomato sauce
- 3 1/2 cups vegetable broth
- 2 tsp garlic, minced
- 1 jalapeno pepper, diced
- 1 bell pepper, seeded and chopped
- 1 cup onion, chopped
- 2 tbsp olive oil
- 1/2 tsp salt

Directions:

1. Add oil into the instant pot and select sauté.
2. Add onion, jalapeno, and bell pepper in hot oil and sauté for 2-3 minutes.
3. Add garlic and sauté for a minute. Add remaining ingredients and stir to combine.
4. Seal pot with lid and select manual high pressure for 25 minutes.
5. Allow to release pressure naturally then open the lid.

6. Stir well and serve.

Nutrition information:

Calories per serving: 277; Carbohydrates: 5.7g; Protein: 15.7g; Fat: 5.7g; Sugar: 4.4g; Sodium: 657mg; Fiber: 10.8g

Perfect Baked Beans

(Total Time: 1 hour 25 Min| Serves: 10)

Ingredients

- 1 lb dry navy beans, rinsed and drained
- 4 garlic cloves, minced
- 1 tbsp olive oil
- 1 onion, chopped
- 2 tsp hot sauce
- 1 1/2 tbsp Worcestershire sauce
- 2 tbsp apple cider vinegar
- 3/4 cup ketchup
- 1/2 cup brown sugar
- 3/4 cup molasses

- 3/4 tsp salt

Directions:

1. Add water and beans into the instant pot. Seal pot with lid and select bean setting and set timer for 60 minutes.
2. Allow to release pressure naturally then open the lid.
3. Drain beans and set aside.
4. Add oil into the instant pot and select sauté.
5. Add garlic and onion and sauté for 2-3 minutes.
6. Add cooked beans and remaining ingredients into the instant pot and stir well to combine.
7. Seal pot with lid and select bean setting and set timer for 15 minutes.
8. Allow to release pressure naturally then open the lid.
9. Stir well and serve.

Nutrition information:

Calories per serving: 290; Carbohydrates: 59.5g; Protein: 10.7g; Fat: 2.2g; Sugar: 27.5g; Sodium: 439mg; Fiber: 11.4g

Chili Lime Black Beans

(Total Time: 60 Min| Serves: 6)

Ingredients

- 2 cups dry black beans, rinsed and drained
- 3 cups water
- 1 tsp paprika
- 1 tbsp chili powder
- 4 garlic cloves, minced
- 2 tsp olive oil
- 1 onion, chopped
- 1 fresh lime juice
- 1 tsp salt

Directions:

1. Add oil into the instant pot and select sauté.
2. Add onion and garlic in hot oil and sauté until softened.
3. Add beans, paprika, chili powder, water, and salt. Stir well.
4. Seal pot with lid and select manual and set timer for 50 minutes.
5. Allow to release pressure naturally then open the lid.

6. Add lime juice and stir well.

7. Serve and enjoy.

Nutrition information:

Calories per serving: 251; Carbohydrates: 44.2g; Protein: 14.5g; Fat: 2.8g; Sugar: 2.4g; Sodium: 408mg; Fiber: 10.9g

Simple Black Bean Chili

(Total Time: 40 Min| Serves: 4)

Ingredients

- 1 cup water
- 1 jalapeno pepper, minced
- 15 oz can tomatoes, crushed
- 15 oz can black beans, drained
- 2 tsp ground cumin
- 2 tbsp chili powder
- 2 garlic cloves, minced
- 1 tsp dried oregano
- 1 bell pepper, diced

- 1 medium onion, diced
- 2 tsp olive oil
- 1 tsp kosher salt

Directions:

1. Add olive oil into the instant pot and select sauté.
2. Add onion, oregano, and bell pepper in hot oil and sauté for 7 minutes.
3. Add garlic, cumin, and chili powder and stir for a minute.
4. Add beans, jalapeno, tomatoes, water, and salt. Stir well.
5. Seal pot with lid and select manual high pressure for 5 minutes.
6. Release pressure using quick release method than open the lid.
7. Stir well and serve.

Nutrition information:

Calories per serving: 181; Carbohydrates: 32.5g; Protein: 8.1g; Fat: 0.5g; Sugar: 7.6g; Sodium: 1244mg; Fiber: 9.4g

Tomatillo White Beans

(Total Time: 50 Min| Serves: 6)

Ingredients

- 1 1/2 cups dry great northern beans, soaked in water for overnight, rinsed and drained
- 2 tsp dried oregano
- 1 1/2 cups water
- 1 1/2 tsp ground cumin
- 1/2 jalapeno, chopped
- 1 cup onion, chopped
- 1 cup poblano, remove seeds and chopped
- 2 cup tomatillos, chopped
- Pepper
- Salt

Directions:

1. Add tomatillos, jalapeno, onion, and poblano into the blender and blend until vegetable is in tiny pieces.
2. Pour blender vegetables into the instant pot and select sauté.
3. Add ground cumin and stir well. Sauté vegetable mixture for 4 minutes.

4. Add beans, oregano, and water. Stir well.
5. Seal pot with lid and select manual high pressure for 35 minutes.
6. Allow to release pressure naturally then open the lid.
7. Season with pepper and salt.
8. Serve and enjoy.

Nutrition information:

Calories per serving: 226; Carbohydrates: 44.2g; Protein: 13.5g; Fat: 0.2g; Sugar: 1.9g; Sodium: 40mg; Fiber: 18.8g

Chipotle Black Beans

(Total Time: 45 Min| Serves: 4)

Ingredients

- 1 cup dry black beans, rinsed and drained
- 1 tsp chipotle powder
- 1 tsp paprika
- 2 tsp cumin powder

- 3 cups vegetable broth
- 3 garlic cloves, minced
- 1 tbsp olive oil
- 1/2 onion, diced

Directions:

1. Add oil into the instant pot and select sauté.
2. Add garlic and onion in hot oil and sauté for 5 minutes.
3. Add broth, water, spices, and black beans. Stir well.
4. Seal pot with lid and select Bean/chili setting and set timer for 35 minutes.
5. Allow to release pressure naturally then open the lid.
6. Serve and enjoy.

Nutrition information:

Calories per serving: 239; Carbohydrates: 33.7g; Protein: 14.7g; Fat: 5.5g; Sugar: 2.2g; Sodium: 578mg; Fiber: 8g

Simple Garlicky Pinto Beans

(Total Time: 60 Min| Serves: 12)

Ingredients

- 1 lb dry pinto beans, rinsed and drained
- 2 tsp onion powder
- 2 garlic cloves, minced
- 5 cups vegetable broth
- 1 tsp black pepper
- 1 tsp chili powder
- 2 tsp salt

Directions:

1. Add all ingredients into the instant pot and stir well.
2. Seal pot with lid and select manual and set the timer for 55 minutes.
3. Release pressure using quick release method than open the lid.
4. Serve and enjoy.

Nutrition information:

Calories per serving: 150; Carbohydrates: 24.8g; Protein: 10.2g; Fat: 1.1g; Sugar: 1.3g; Sodium: 713mg; Fiber: 6g

Black Eyed Peas with Collard Greens
(Total Time: 20 Min| Serves: 6)

Ingredients

- 1 cup dried black-eyed peas, rinsed and drained
- 6 garlic cloves, minced
- 1 onion, chopped
- 4 cups collard greens, cut into pieces
- 1 tsp liquid smoke
- 1 tsp hot sauce
- 2 tbsp apple cider vinegar
- 1 tsp thyme
- 2 bay leaves
- 1 tsp red pepper flakes
- 2 cups water
- 1 tsp pepper
- 1 tsp salt

Directions:

1. Add all ingredients except vinegar, liquid smoke, and hot sauce into the instant pot and stir well.
2. Seal pot with lid and select manual high pressure for 10 minutes.

3. Allow to release pressure naturally then open the lid.
4. Add hot sauce, liquid smoke, and vinegar and stir well.
5. Serve and enjoy.

Nutrition information:

Calories per serving: 54; Carbohydrates: 10.3g; Protein: 3.1g; Fat: 0.6g; Sugar: 0.9g; Sodium: 426mg; Fiber: 3g

SAUCES & MORE

Simple Applesauce

(Total Time: 40 Min| Serves: 8)

Ingredients

- 3 lbs apples, peeled, cored, and sliced
- 1 cinnamon stick
- 1 tbsp apple cider vinegar
- 1/4 cup water

Directions:

1. Add all ingredients into the instant pot and stir well.
2. Seal pot with lid and select manual high pressure for 30 minutes.
3. Release pressure using quick release method than open the lid.
4. Discard cinnamon stick. Transfer apple mixture into the blender and blend until smooth.
5. Serve and enjoy.

Nutrition information:

Calories per serving: 44; Carbohydrates: 11.6g; Protein: 0.2g; Fat: 0.2g; Sugar: 8.7g; Sodium: 1mg; Fiber: 2g

Creamy Cauliflower Alfredo Sauce

(Total Time: 20 Min| Serves: 6)

Ingredients

- 1 cauliflower head, cut into florets
- 2 tsp garlic powder
- 1 tsp onion powder
- 1/4 cup half and half
- 1 cup vegetable broth
- 4 garlic cloves, minced
- 2 tbsp butter
- 1 tsp salt

Directions:

1. Add butter into the instant pot and select sauté.
2. Add garlic and sauté for minutes.
3. Add cauliflower and broth. Stir well. Seal pot with lid and select manual high pressure for 6 minutes.
4. Allow to release pressure naturally then open the lid.
5. Transfer cauliflower mixture into the blender along with garlic powder, onion powder, and salt and blend until smooth.

6. Add half and half and stir well.

7. Serve and enjoy.

Nutrition information:

Calories per serving: 72; Carbohydrates: 4.6g; Protein: 2.4g; Fat: 5.3g; Sugar: 1.6g; Sodium: 560mg; Fiber: 1.3g

Quick Cheesy Sauce

(Total Time: 25 Min| Serves: 8)

Ingredients

- 2 cups water
- 1 tbsp turmeric
- 1/2 cup nutritional yeast
- 1/2 cup cashews
- 3 garlic cloves, peeled
- 1/2 cup onion, chopped
- 1 cup carrots, chopped
- 2 cups potato, peeled and chopped
- 1 tsp salt

Directions:

1. Add all ingredients into the instant pot and stir to combine.
2. Seal pot with lid and select manual and set timer for 5 minutes.
3. Release pressure using quick release method than open the lid.
4. Using blender blend until smooth and creamy.
5. Serve and enjoy.

Nutrition information:

Calories per serving: 100; Carbohydrates: 12.1g; Protein: 5.9g; Fat: 4.1g; Sugar: 1.4g; Sodium: 278mg; Fiber: 3.5g

Vanilla Applesauce
(Total Time: 25 Min| Serves: 12)

Ingredients

- 2 lbs golden delicious apples, cored and diced

- 2 lbs Fuji apples, cored and diced
- 1/4 tsp ground cardamom
- 1 tbsp ground cinnamon
- 2 tsp vanilla extract
- 1 cup water
- 1 lb granny smith apples, cored and diced
- 1/4 tsp kosher salt

Directions:

1. Add all ingredients into the instant pot and stir well.
2. Seal pot with lid and select manual high pressure for 7 minutes.
3. Allow to release pressure naturally then open the lid.
4. Using blender blend until smooth and creamy.
5. Pour applesauce in an airtight container.
6. Store in refrigerator and serve.

Nutrition information:

Calories per serving: 82; Carbohydrates: 21.9g; Protein: 0.1g; Fat: 0.1g; Sugar: 16.5g; Sodium: 51mg; Fiber: 4.9g

Caramel Sauce
(Total Time: 25 Min| Serves: 8)

Ingredients

- 1/3 cup heavy cream
- 1/2 tsp vanilla extract
- 3 tbsp butter
- 1/3 cup water
- 1 cup sugar
- 1/2 tsp sea salt

Directions:

1. Add water and sugar into the instant pot and select sauté. Stir well and cook for 14 minutes.
2. After 14 minutes add heavy cream and butter and stir until smooth.
3. Add vanilla and salt and stir well.
4. Turn off the instant pot and pour sauce in glass jar and place in refrigerator.
5. Serve and enjoy.

Nutrition information:

Calories per serving: 150; Carbohydrates: 25.2g; Protein: 0.2g; Fat: 3.9g; Sugar: 25g; Sodium: 150mg; Fiber: 0g

Easy Cranberry Sauce

(Total Time: 15 Min| Serves: 8)

Ingredients

- 1/4 cup orange juice
- 1 tsp orange zest
- 1/2 cup maple syrup
- 12 oz cranberries

Directions:

1. Add all ingredients into the instant pot and stir well.
2. Seal pot with lid and select manual high pressure for 5 minutes.
3. Allow to release pressure naturally then open the lid.
4. Using wooden spoon mash berries lightly. Pour sauce in glass jar and store in the refrigerator.
5. Serve and enjoy.

Nutrition information:

Calories per serving: 78; Carbohydrates: 18g; Protein: 0.1g; Fat: 0.1g; Sugar: 13.9g; Sodium: 2mg; Fiber: 1.6g

Healthy Strawberry Applesauce
(Total Time: 25 Min| Serves: 12)

Ingredients

- 8 apples, peeled, cored, and sliced
- 2 tbsp fresh lemon juice
- 1/4 tsp cinnamon
- 2 cups frozen strawberries
- 1/4 cup sugar
- 1 pear, peeled, cored, and sliced

Directions:

1. Add all ingredients into the instant pot and stir well.
2. Seal pot with lid and select manual high pressure for 5 minutes.
3. Allow to release pressure naturally then open the lid.
4. Transfer sauce content into the blender and blend until smooth.
5. Serve and enjoy.

Nutrition information:

Calories per serving: 109; Carbohydrates: 28.7g; Protein: 0.5g; Fat: 0.3g; Sugar: 22.3g; Sodium: 2mg; Fiber: 4.5g

Yummy Strawberry Jam

(Total Time: 20 Min| Serves: 8)

Ingredients

- 3 cup strawberries
- 1 tbsp cornstarch
- 1 tbsp water
- 2 tbsp fresh lemon juice
- 3/4 cup sugar

Directions:

1. Add strawberries, lemon juice, and sugar into the instant pot and stir well.

2. Seal pot with lid and select manual high pressure for 3 minutes.

3. Allow to release pressure naturally then open the lid.

4. Mix together water and cornstarch and pour into the instant pot. Stir well.

5. Pour jam in air-tight container and store in the refrigerator.

6. Serve and enjoy.

Nutrition information:

Calories per serving: 92; Carbohydrates: 23.9g; Protein: 0.4g; Fat: 0.2g; Sugar: 21.5g; Sodium: 1mg; Fiber: 1.1g

Blueberry Jam

(Total Time: 15 Min| Serves: 8)

Ingredients

- 2 cups blueberries
- 1 tbsp chia seeds

- 2 tbsp maple syrup

Directions:

1. Add blueberries and maple syrup into the instant pot. Stir well.
2. Seal pot with lid and select manual high pressure for 2 minutes.
3. Allow to release pressure naturally then open the lid.
4. Add chia seeds and stir well. Using blender blend sauce until get desired consistency.
5. Pour sauce in air-tight container and store in the refrigerator.
6. Serve and enjoy.

Nutrition information:

Calories per serving: 53; Carbohydrates: 9.9g; Protein: 1.1g; Fat: 1.3g; Sugar: 6.6g; Sodium: 1mg; Fiber: 2.2g

Rosemary Applesauce
(Total Time: 25 Min| Serves: 8)

Ingredients

- 3 lbs apples, peeled, cored and chopped
- 2 tsp pie spice
- 1/2 cup coconut sugar
- 1 fresh rosemary sprig
- 1/2 cup apple juice

Directions:

1. Add all ingredients into the instant pot and stir to combine.
2. Seal pot with lid and select manual high pressure for 5 minutes.
3. Allow to release pressure naturally then open the lid.
4. Discard rosemary sprig. Using blender blend until smooth.
5. Pour sauce in air-tight container and store in the refrigerator.
6. Serve and enjoy.

Nutrition information:

Calories per serving: 58; Carbohydrates: 14.8g; Protein: 0.3g; Fat: 0.2g; Sugar: 10.2g; Sodium: 4mg; Fiber: 2.1g

DESSERTS

Gluten-Free Rice Pudding
(Total Time: 30 Min| Serves: 4)

Ingredients

- 1 1/2 cups almond milk
- 1/2 tsp ground nutmeg
- 2 tsp ground cinnamon
- 1 tsp vanilla extract
- 3/4 cup brown rice
- 1 cup water
- 1/8 tsp sea salt

Directions:

1. Add rice, cinnamon, nutmeg, vanilla, water, almond milk, and salt into the instant pot and stir well.
2. Seal pot with lid and select porridge setting and set timer for 20 minutes.
3. Allow to release pressure naturally then open the lid.
4. Stir well and serve.

Nutrition information:

Calories per serving: 343; Carbohydrates: 33.3g; Protein: 4.8g; Fat: 22.5g; Sugar: 3.2g; Sodium: 75mg; Fiber: 3.9g

Cranberry Coconut Pudding
(Total Time: 30 Min| Serves: 6)

Ingredients

- 1 cup brown rice, rinsed and drained
- 2 tsp stevia
- 1/2 tsp cinnamon
- 1/2 cup water
- 1/2 cup coconut milk
- 1 1/2 cups milk
- 1 cup cranberries

Directions:

1. Add all ingredients into the instant pot and stir well.
2. Seal pot with lid and select porridge setting and set timer for 20 minutes.

3. Allow to release pressure naturally then open the lid.
4. Stir well and serve.

Nutrition information:

Calories per serving: 202; Carbohydrates: 30.1g; Protein: 4.9g; Fat: 6.9g; Sugar: 4.1g; Sodium: 34mg; Fiber: 2.3g

Delicious Tapioca Pudding

(Total Time: 25 Min| Serves: 4)

Ingredients

- 1/2 cup small pearl tapioca
- 1 can coconut milk
- 1 cup almond milk
- 1/2 cup water
- 1/4 cup maple syrup

Directions:

1. In a bowl, soak tapioca pearls in almond milk for 1 hour.
2. Combine together all ingredients except water into the oven-safe bowl.

3. Cover bowl with foil. Pour 1/2 cup water into the instant pot the place trivet into the pot.
4. Place bowl on a trivet. Seal pot with lid and select manual high pressure for 8 minutes.
5. Allow to release pressure naturally then open the lid.
6. Stir well and place in refrigerator.
7. Serve and enjoy.

Nutrition information:

Calories per serving: 301; Carbohydrates: 37.3g; Protein: 1.7g; Fat: 17.3g; Sugar: 13.7g; Sodium: 19mg; Fiber: 1.3g

Easy Baked Apples

(Total Time: 15 Min| Serves: 6)

Ingredients

- 6 medium apples, peeled, cored, and sliced
- 2 tbsp cinnamon
- 1/2 cup sugar
- 1 cup apple juice

Directions:

1. Add apple slices into the instant pot.

2. Sprinkle sugar and cinnamon on top of apple slices.
3. Pour apple juice over the apple slices. Seal pot with lid and select manual and set timer for 8 minutes.
4. Allow to release pressure naturally then open the lid.
5. Serve hot and enjoy.

Nutrition information:

Calories per serving: 203; Carbohydrates: 54g; Protein: 0.7g; Fat: 0.5g; Sugar: 43.9g; Sodium: 4mg; Fiber: 6.7g

Bread Pudding

(Total Time: 30 Min| Serves: 4)

Ingredients

- 3 eggs, beaten
- 1 tsp coconut oil
- 1/2 tsp vanilla
- 4 cup bread cube
- 1 tsp cinnamon
- 1/2 cup raisins

- 1 cup milk
- 1 cup coconut milk
- 1/4 tsp salt

Directions:

1. Pour water into the instant pot then place trivet into the pot.
2. Add bread cubes in casserole dish.
3. In a large bowl, mix together remaining ingredients until well combined.
4. Pour the mixture into the instant pot on top of bread cubes and cover dish with aluminum foil.
5. Place casserole dish on a trivet. Seal pot with lid and select steam setting and set timer for 15 minutes.
6. Allow to release pressure naturally then open the lid.
7. Remove casserole dish carefully from the instant pot.
8. Serve warm and enjoy.

Nutrition information:

Calories per serving: 376; Carbohydrates: 39.2g; Protein: 10.8g; Fat: 21.2g; Sugar: 17.3g; Sodium: 472mg; Fiber: 3.1g

Chocolate Rice Pudding

(Total Time: 30 Min| Serves: 6)

Ingredients

- 2 eggs, beaten
- 1 tsp vanilla
- 5 cups coconut milk
- 1 cup rice, rinsed
- 1 tbsp coconut oil
- 1 cup coconut sugar
- 2 tbsp cocoa powder

Directions:

1. Add all ingredients into the instant pot and select sauté mode. Stir constantly and bring to boil.
2. Seal pot with lid and select rice setting.
3. Allow to release pressure naturally then open the lid.
4. Stir well and serve.

Nutrition information:

Calories per serving: 279; Carbohydrates: 31.4g; Protein: 5.7g; Fat: 14.2g; Sugar: 0.3g; Sodium: 53mg; Fiber: 0.9g

Delicious Brownie Cake

(Total Time: 35 Min| Serves: 6)

Ingredients

- 2 eggs
- 1/3 cup cocoa powder
- 1/2 tsp baking powder
- 1/3 cup all-purpose flour
- 4 tbsp butter
- 1 cup water
- 1/3 cup pecans, chopped
- 1/3 cup chocolate chips
- 1/3 cup sugar
- 1/8 tsp salt

Directions:

1. In a mixing bowl, whisk together butter, cocoa powder, baking powder, flour, eggs, sugar, and salt.
2. Add pecans and chocolate chips into the batter and fold well.
3. Pour batter into the 6-inch pan and cover with aluminum foil piece.
4. Pour water into the instant pot and place trivet into the pot.

5. Place cake pan on a trivet. Seal pot with lid and select manual and set timer for 20 minutes.
6. Allow to release pressure naturally for 10 minutes then release using quick release method.
7. Cut brownie cake into pieces and serve.

Nutrition information:

Calories per serving: 263; Carbohydrates: 25.8g; Protein: 4.9g; Fat: 17.5g; Sugar: 16.4g; Sodium: 135mg; Fiber: 2.6g

Yummy Chocolate Mousse

(Total Time: 30 Min| Serves: 5)

Ingredients

- 4 egg yolks
- 1 cup whipping cream
- 1/2 cup cocoa powder
- 1/4 cup water
- 1/2 cup Swerve
- 1/2 tsp vanilla
- 1/2 cup almond milk
- 1/4 tsp sea salt

Directions:

1. Whisk egg yolk in a mixing bowl.
2. In a saucepan, add cocoa, water and swerve and whisk over medium heat until sugar is melted.
3. Add almond milk and cream to the saucepan and whisk to combine. Do not boil the mixture.
4. Add vanilla and salt and stir well.
5. Pour mixture into the ramekins.
6. Pour 1 1/2 cups water into the instant pot then place a trivet in the pot.
7. Place ramekins on a trivet. Seal pot with lid and select manual and set timer for 6 minutes.
8. Release pressure using quick release method than open the lid.
9. Serve and enjoy.

Nutrition information:

Calories per serving: 189; Carbohydrates: 31.3g; Protein: 4.8g; Fat: 17.9g; Sugar: 25.1g; Sodium: 114mg; Fiber: 3.1g

Sweet Coconut Almond Risotto

(Total Time: 25 Min| Serves: 4)

Ingredients

- 1/3 cup coconut sugar

- 1 cup Arborio rice
- 1 cup coconut milk
- 2 cups almond milk
- 1/4 cup coconut flakes
- 2 tsp vanilla extract

Directions:

1. Add coconut and almond milk into the instant pot and select sauté. Stir well and bring to boil.
2. Add rice and stir well. Seal pot with lid and select manual high pressure for 5 minutes.
3. Allow to release pressure naturally then open the lid.
4. Add coconut sugar and vanilla extract and stir well.
5. Top with coconut flakes and serve.

Nutrition information:

Calories per serving: 361; Carbohydrates: 44.7g; Protein: 5.3g; Fat: 18g; Sugar: 2.6g; Sodium: 107mg; Fiber: 3.6g

Easy Blueberry Muffins

(Total Time: 35 Min| Serves: 6)

Ingredients

- 2 eggs
- 1/4 cup sour cream
- 1/4 cup almond milk
- 1 cup sugar
- 1/4 cup butter, softened
- 1/2 tsp baking soda
- 1 tsp baking powder
- 1 tsp vanilla extract
- 1/2 lemon juice
- 1 lemon zest
- 1/2 cup fresh blueberries
- 1 cup all-purpose flour
- 1/4 tsp salt

Directions:

1. Add all ingredients into the mixing bowl and mix well.
2. Pour batter into the 6 silicone mold.
3. Pour 1 cup water into the instant pot then place trivet into the pot.
4. Place muffins mold on a trivet. Seal pot with lid and select manual high pressure for 25 minutes.
5. Allow to release pressure naturally then open the lid.
6. Serve and enjoy.

Nutrition information:

Calories per serving: 344; Carbohydrates: 52.6g; Protein: 4.7g; Fat: 13.8g; Sugar: 35.2g; Sodium: 285mg; Fiber: 1.1g

Made in the USA
Monee, IL
03 December 2019